the
chaos
of longing

k.y. robinson

Andrews McMeel
PUBLISHING®

to those who
lie awake
burning.

Trigger Warning

This book contains descriptions of sexual trauma,
suicidal ideation, racism, and sexism.
Please exercise discretion and healthy self-care.

contents

inception

blood

i'm half jerk chicken
and collard greens
suffocating
in this nightmare
called the american dream.

faada

he only said
he loved me
when i was being
reprimanded.
that's when i learned
i had to tempt chaos
to feel loved.

mother's nature

i used to
turn away
from her
but now
i'm turning
into her
slowly
like honey.

deferred

i can't pinpoint
the moment
my father realized
america wasn't
what he thought
it would be.
he quelled
his rage with beer
and took up residence
on the bathroom floor
to regurgitate all the ache.

i can't pinpoint
the moment
when my mother
couldn't bring herself
to utter or accept an
"i love you."
so i carved
my own version of love
into the flesh of men.
to feel their heat rising.
to keep me
from unearthing
my predisposition
for shrinking.

i can't pinpoint
the moment
we decided to stay
in the sun too long
and made raisins
of ourselves.
we sucked the juice
out of ourselves
and withered
on the vine
called life.

fast tailed girl

in their famished eyes,
we were prey.
women we thought we had
a few more years to meet.

it was an unjust
rite of passage
for girls whose bodies
were full as oceans
with waves that didn't fit
quietly in an hourglass.

time ran out on our
carefree girlhood.
our bodies ceased
belonging to us.
every wandering eye
became the highest bidder.

boys grabbed
our blooming bodies
and gave no regard
to our withering petals.

men who were old enough
to be our fathers
waited for our ripe bodies
to fall from our mothers' trees
as if they were entitled to
our fruit.

we began to resent
the womanly stranger
extending from our bodies.
others did too.
we were fast tailed girls for
garnering unwanted attention.

we wanted to shrink
into ourselves
and become invisible.
we just wanted to be children.

13

i was an insecure
cocoa brown
hunchback girl
who swallowed poems
and never thought of
heaven or hell
when i met him.
i was thirteen
cursed with acne
and overripe breasts
longing to feel pretty.

he was twice my age,
a smooth talker,
and towered over me
like sugarcane.

in time i learned
he wasn't so sweet.

in time i learned
that my body and soul
would become casualties
of an unholy war where
god never came
but he did.

magic

she has an air
about her
that suffocates
women like me
who are the epitome
of insecurity.

she stores magic
in her cheeks
and runs up a tree
when i ask for a piece.

i guess it's up to me
to find my own.
maybe i'll find some
on the way home.

broken

i feel like something
is broken inside of me like:
shattered glass,
cracked eggs
on the kitchen floor,
brittle twigs
in the dead of winter,
and shards of a mirror
that said i would never be
the fairest of them all.

manic depression

one moment life
is more pigmented
than technicolor.
glitter flows
through my veins
and the stars
in my eyes dilate
and burst
into delusions.

minutes, hours,
or days later,
shades of blue and black
surround me like smoke.
the glitter morphs
into shards of glass
and taunts every
breath that i take.

14

i mastered the art of suffocating
without drowning.
i learned how
to numb myself as
his sweaty
mammoth body
straddled me
in depraved delight.
but i never mastered
the art of forgetting.
remembrance
remains etched
on my bones.

faithless

you are the elephant
in the room
that i won't acknowledge
and am too afraid to poach.
my faith has always quivered
and never learned the beauty
of stillness and there are times
i want to press my hands
against each other like lovers
and evict all doubts
but i always end up
with more questions
than answers.

17

the third time
isn't always a charm.

it can be a curse that
hollows you out
after he's gutted
what's left of you.

after you're left alone
with a vulture perched
at the door waiting
to feed on you next.

and at that moment,
you're not thinking about
what your boyfriend
has done to you.

you're grateful
for doors that lock.
you're grateful
it wasn't kicked down.
you're grateful when
he returns two hours later.

stigma & shame

i carry all my hurt
like satchels.
i can only unpack
them on pages.

despair climbed
out of my throat
when i wasn't looking
and fell on my lap.

i wanted to jump
from my bones
and disperse
in the wind
like dandelion
seed heads.
to be free
and light as air.

i wanted to feel
the hot air of
anticipating mouths
bidding me farewell
as the wind carried me
into the next life.

now i'm alone
in a cold gated room
that engulfed
and mocked me
because i opened
my mouth
instead of
writing a poem.

this stigma.
this shame.
is stifling.

open season

i am afraid
to have a child.

i am afraid
their black body
will be considered
an unholy land.

the bass or sass
in their voice
will be heard as
a war cry.

the sun will
pack up and leave
their eyes.

i am afraid
there will be nothing
i can do or say
to relieve the burden
of blackness.

women like me

we are the abandoned houses
of the world—
stripped of our humanity,
femininity, and autonomy.

rocks are thrown
at the windows of our souls.
we're expected to stand stoically
and dare not flinch.

our magic is considered
anything but soft.
it is neck rolling,
finger snapping,
and has teeth.

we aren't the doe-eyed
saving kind.
we are supposed to gather
our wounds in silence,
disinfect them, and heal
all on our own.

longing

you'll get used to me

it will not be love
at first sight
when you look at me.
your eyes and heart
must adjust to me.
darkness lives here.

i will not fit perfectly.
you'll have to break me in
like brand new shoes
and i will pinch you
with every step.

i will grow on you
like weeds
in an untended garden.
you'll yank me out
in hopes that something
beautiful will sprout
in my place
but it never does.

i will slowly seep
into the floorboards
of your heart
until they squeak
and buckle.
this will be your new home
and you cannot afford to leave.
i won't let you.

naked thoughts

i stand naked
before you.
i fear you may
see my heart.
i'm not well
with the secrets
my body tells.

the truth is
complicated.
it's easier to lie
and spread
my legs apart.

it is easier to push
your head lower
than to say
what's going on
inside my head.

it is easier to say
"make love to me"
than to say
*"love me
and only me."*

star eater

when you look at me,
stars cluster in your eyes
but i often wonder if
my black holes
will swallow them whole
because deep down
i'm a connoisseur
of sabotage.

dear future lover

teach me how to love
without running
with my eyes shut.

teach me how to love
without filling
hollow hearts
until i've become
a shell of myself.

teach me how to love
without becoming
a land mine
on the inside.

teach me that love
is not war
but peacetime
in your eyes.

blood diamond

i yield to you
like you're the answer
to my savagery
because no one
explores my body
the way you do.

you dig so deep.
i don't know
what you're looking
for and i hope
you never find it.

i haven't found
myself yet and i know
it's in your bloodline
to colonize and exploit
untapped resources.

forbidden fruit

i crave to press
my teeth against
your ripeness
and feel your kisses
burst in my mouth
like summer berries
just before the poison
sets in.

melanin

i love your smile
and the metaphors
it rebukes and represents.
your sting is so sweet.
i am drunk off the honey
of your africanized being.
you are the manifestation
of the ancestors.

your skin is dark
as the velvet night.
your starred eyes
are tenants in constellations.
even the moon swells
whenever you're near.

you are all the makings
of love at first sight.
when i dream of you,
i will hold you hostage
underneath my eyelids.

poetry

i compose my love
for you in stanzas
knowing where to
break us.

i lie in bed
with pen
and paper
because it never
puts on
its clothes
and leaves—

even when
i struggle
to write
the next line.

until you

i never believed in serenity
until i felt your breath
on the nape of my neck
evaporating the chaos
crawling on my skin.

i never believed in prayer
until i started loving you
and asked every god
i could conjure up
for you to love me back.

i never believed in heaven
until i felt every star aligned
across your skin.
you are a galaxy within
my graceless grasp.

sun & moon

i carry the sun
in my mouth.
i know how to
lure you away
from the twilight
and make you rise
over my horizon.

you carry the moon
on your body.
you know how to
make me howl like a wolf
and lull me to sleep.

cathedral

your mouth
is a cathedral.
i want to fall
to my knees
and repent for past,
present,
and future sins
just to part them
and taste a piece
of your heaven.

oyster

as i dive for pearls,
place them
in my mouth
and hand me
a warm washcloth
for the ones
that escaped.

electric bodies

i can smell
what makes you a man
from across the room.
it boils my blood
to an electric blue
and engulfs my mouth
with desire.

plug yourself inside.
feel the electricity
traveling through
our circuits.

summon the
ravenous beast
kneeling inside
aching to be freed
through the small
of my back.

arithmetic

you are the sum
of my lust.
subtracted
of reasoning.
divided by
my legs.
multiplied by
your thrusts.
you dilate
my third eye.
send shivers down
my inner thigh.
i smell you
in my dreams.
being more
than platonic
but erotic
human beings.

garden

i trembled
on the vine
waiting to be
sampled by you.
the fruit of my flesh
unpeeled in complete surrender.
put your mouth on me.
break me open.
have a taste of paradise.

beautiful stranger

if i could fall in the abyss
i would capture your bliss
and grant you affection
i will no longer
ache for your lips
or lose my direction.

peel layers of me
i've never seen
turn me inside out
make the earth sprout
from underneath me.

i feel spellbound
when you surround
and rush through my veins
i want to lose myself
until nothing's the same
in ecstasy's name.

uncensored

i want to caress you
with the flesh
of my words
until you are found
naked,
breathless,
and too overwhelmed
to read the next line.

i want to push you
against the wall
of my words.
pin you down,
deprive you
of sight,
and trace
each letter
across your lips.

thrust your eyes
against my pages.
repeat with me
until you surrender
to love's doctrine.

transference

there's midnight
in his skin.
he even smells
like you.
an ache begins
to rise
in my bones.
i want to
close my eyes
and pretend
he's you
for a while.

longing

what should i do
with this longing?
tuck it away like a letter
i'm too afraid to send?

hold it deep inside
another man's desire
and pray i don't scream
out your name?

denounce it like a sin
and excommunicate
the heat rising
inside me?
you have not traveled
in my longing
and been stranded
on the corner of
unspoken words
and telltale stares.

you'll never collapse
under the weight of it
and remain suspended
in the air by a kiss
that will never
touch your lips.

sponge

in the damp dark,
you were the sponge
soaking up my lonely.

residues

i am reminded
of your heat
when another man
touches me.
he brushes
off the embers
you once left behind.
i still burn for you.

hunger

your appetite
for me
is seasonal.

my longing
for you
is relentless.

meal

you reminded me
of the salt fish stew
that my father made.
you tasted like home but
i resented the bones
you made me choke on.

when flour,
baking powder,
salt, and water
were pressed down
by strong palms
and fried in oil
that raged
like a revolution,
all was forgiven.
i devoured you.

metamorphic

dark cocoons
line my heart but
when i look at you,
butterflies flutter
and give birth
to spring.

beekeeper

put your mouth
on places
forbidden
to speak.
harvest
the honey
that only
drips for you.

inebriated

write me love letters
dripping with the blood
from your fermented heart.
i want to get drunk
off your words
and become undone
like ribbons
with each and
every syllable.

poetry ii

i can already
smell
and taste
the ways
you'll hurt me.

stay
away
from
me.

or you'll
become my
next muse.

love at first sight

the first time i saw you,
you siphoned the air
out of the room
and left me breathless.
i thought you were god.

for you

i would lasso the sun
and sell her rays
for profit
so you wouldn't
be blinded
by her anymore.

i would eat
all the stars
just for you to see
light in my eyes.

i would bounce
my love off rainclouds
just to soften
your calcified heart.

what are you willing
to do for me?

the good guy

i am good at holding
onto nothing
like it's all i have
and running away
from something real
like it's the plague.

i don't think
i deserve you
so i grasp at straws
instead of pressing
my lips against
the glass of your being
and slowly taking a sip.

i don't have
much to bring
but a broken heart
that feeds on flesh
and poetry.

i'll disappoint you
because it's all i know.

one wish

if you told me
to come to you
right now
i would drop
everything,
watch it shatter
like glass,
and crawl
on the broken pieces
to show you
how much
love hurts.

entrails

i already know
how to set
your body on fire
and watch the trail
of ashes smolder but
i want to learn
how to find
a place in your heart.

path

i took the
scenic route
to your heart
and got lost
in your kiss.

elements

i search for water
in your mouth,
fire in your eyes,
earth on your body,
and wind when you
whisper in my ear.

smitten

i love losing myself
inside of you.
i am too smitten
by your landscape
to retrace my steps
or ask for directions.

i want to stay here
for a while
before reality
sets in.

tone deaf

we were
predestined
to align.
play and rewind.
asked to define
a love supreme,
malignant,
or benign.

don't string
me along
but love me
like music.

my song
is as sweet
as hers
if you would
only listen.

but you sever
the chord
and chain
our melodies.

i believe
it is her song
that clouds
your ears.

nocturnal melody

i burn for you in the dark—
unable to separate
the moon from the stars.

you have enchanted my night
despite rumors of your
infatuation with the sun.

your eclipsed heart
will wail for my stars
until you realize
you need
my cosmic grace.

chaos

charcoal

if the root
of all suffering
is attachment,
i see why
i'm drawn
to unavailable men.

post-vacation blues

i wish i knew what i did
that sent them running
for the hills
after they've nestled
in my valley,
pinched and raised
my mountain peaks,
and made rivers
erupt from me.
sometimes i wonder if
i'm too much rainfall
and not enough sun.

unthreaded

i can tell by the look
in your eyes
that tomorrow
is hanging
by a thread
and the future
is never winding
onto a spool.

unrequited love

unrequited love
is like kneeling
on uncooked rice
and waiting for
the boiling water
of their kisses
to soften the pain
but they never come.

they only peer
through the window
out of pity,
indifference,
or contempt
while you're trying
to crawl out of a poem
they never wanted you
to write.

springtime

i am nothing
but a season
blooming
and bearing fruit
that you only pick
when you crave
something sweet
and forbidden.

summer fling

you will realize
that i'm more than
sweltering heat.
i am a drought.
a wildfire.
an impending storm
you cannot control.

yard work

my heart
is yellowing
and browning
under your
autumn breath.
stuff me
into the bags
of your eyes
because i can't stop
falling for you.

wintered

i wither and
become bare
for you in the end
and seek a warmth
you're incapable
of giving me.

three's a crowd

you steal glimpses of her
and instantly feel inferior
in her presence. you study her
as if you'll be quizzed later.

her body takes up less space
than yours. you wonder if
yours should too. you wonder
if her skin has more stories
than yours. if her eyes open
and shut the windows of his
soul. if her lips taste like milk
and honey.

if he looks into her eyes when
they make love or takes her
from behind like he does you.
like an animal. if he holds her
closer than a secret but never
hides her behind closed doors.

she looks around the room as
if she can smell your thoughts.
you hold your breath hoping it
would stop your heart from
beating so loudly for him.

you're his dirty little secret
hidden in the basement of his
desire. unused and damp with
wanting. you can't stop
scratching at the door trying to
evict her from the corridors of
his heart.

your nails are bloody and your
screams are useless. you have
awakened a sleeping giant.

you've left him no other choice
but to board up the door and
window. you foolishly stay
and collect dust until a
nostalgic craving rises in his
bones and you always give in.

catacomb

he says that there isn't enough
dirt in the world to bury you
after you've nailed him down
to the crucifix of your
insecurities.

that your heart is a catacomb
full of lovers you've bewitched
with your thighs and snuffed
out with your love.

that you're a witch for
hoarding their bones.
that your morality
is more fluid than any body
of water will ever be.

that you'll always be a
paramour in waiting because
you straddle between ravishing
a man and repelling him.
that men only want your fire.
that you should hold the ice.

you began to crisscross
the words he said
into your skin.
as you prick yourself,
you wonder if loving you
is a beast of a burden.

muse

i am not a woman
of many words
unless they are written.
you are a muse meant
to grace my pen.

words sprout
from my heart
and transport
to your pages.

don't treat them
like they're corrosive.
bind them.
acid-free.
maybe in time
you'll find splendor
in these words.

misogynoirist

he said that women like me
were only good for one thing.

his words cut into my flesh
removed my entrails
and stripped the
yellow, red, and blue
of my being.

i felt invisible.
unlovable.
a petal punctured
by the thorn on his side
even though
we bloomed from
the same concrete.

daddy complex

when the crackle
in your voice
grows loud
with lightning
and thunder,
i stand at attention
and hold my breath.
you sound like my father.
i don't know whether
to curse you
or run to my room.

hypothetical

dear painter,
i am the paint
that aches to drip
from your brush.

but will your soft strokes
leave me bleeding
after you've washed
me away?

dear writer,
i hold onto
every word
pressed against
your pages.

if ink dripped
from your fingertips
and i rendered
my body as paper,
would you write
a poem for me?

secret lovers

you treat me as if
you barely know
the scent
of my skin,
the scorch
of my lips
and the grind
of my hips
wantonly
responding
to you.

you treat me as if
i barely know
your hands,
the silk onyx
of your skin,
and the way
you crash
into me
conjuring
the longing
seething underneath
our skin.

stargazer

she's a starry night sky.
you admire her magic
as you thread over me—
never rubbing my earth
between your fingers.

next time tell her
to come down
from unspooling stars
from the moon
to deal with you.

i am tired.

buried

i am not a resting place
for your pleasure.
i bring you back to life.

when life becomes
too heavy
for you to carry,
i absorb the salt
from your veins.

when your tongue
grows bitter,
i grant you my honey.

know this—
you hide more than
your desire
when you're inside of me.

war torn

he had war in his eyes
and waged a rebellion on you.
you arched your back,
parted your lips, and
laid your weapons down
in sheeted surrender.

you've always been a martyr.
you thought you could heal
him from the front line
but you never will.

he is a snake.
he will coil and stiffen
with fangs on standby.
he is threatened by the way
you love him.

heavy

he doesn't say it
but i can tell.

i am too heavy
for him.

my emotions.
my expectations.
this body.
the unsaid words
that hover between us.

he only wants my heavy
when it's hot and
pouring over him.

when it's stretched across
his bed like continents
and doing all the things
that he likes.

then i begin to feel every ocean
form between us.
he's on to the next expedition.
to a land that isn't so dark,
needy, and heavy.

hypocrite

i said i would
leave you alone
and pack what's left
of my heart
and move on.

i said i would
let you be
but conjure
you up
in my dreams.

but on these pages,
you'll always breathe
even though
unrequited love
is suffocating me.

when i found out

when you heard me cry,
did you want to stuff
sand in my eyes
to stop the flood?

did you want to
smother me
in honey to make life
sweet again?

did my pain keep you up
at night?

did it create boulders
in your throat?

probably not.

two halves

don't turn off the lights.
i am drawn to your darkness.
your unspoken emptiness
reminds me of my own.
maybe we can be hollow
together.

pessimist

you showed me
your softer side
and revealed
your petals
but i only waited
to be pricked
by your thorns.

tilted

my love is messy.
it smears on everything
and leaves a stench.

my love is clumsy.
it bumps into everything
and apologizes excessively.

i've yet to find
the equilibrium.

i don't know
how to confine
my love.

caution

when they find out
you have a mental illness,
they'll treat you like glass
and anticipate you breaking
at any given moment.

they'll measure their words
with a pinch of fear
being careful not to overrun
your tiny trembling
cup of sanity.

hoarder

you are a memory
that i fold
and tuck away
because it hurts
too much
to unravel
our history.

but i still can't
manage to throw
you away.
i keep hoping
you'll fit someday.

ghost town

my heart
has become
a tumbleweed
chasing after you.

brokenhearted

once a heart learns
how to break,
it does not know
how to forget.
it endures
sleepless nights,
memorizes
every morsel
of despair,
and relives
every moment
in the stillness
of tears.

last kiss

i am lost
in translation
of our
last kiss.
my lips
have not been
the same.

i've learned
to kiss you
with my eyes.
there are times
you do not see me
as i kiss you
with a quiet desperation
that you would
never understand.

side effect

there's a void
in your eyes
and it hurts
to swim in them.

there is no
reciprocity.
only a lingering
hope and dream
of your love
enveloping me.

tears swell
in the wells
of my eyes.
love is a
constant
side effect
of mine.

resentment

i took an excursion
on your skin,
spun you around,
and molded a
continent of you
but these days
i'm tempted to
push you
over the edge
and watch
you shatter
the same way
you did me.

shameless

you,
the starving artist,
resented
my hunger pains
but continued
to feed on me.

i,
the unrequited lover,
camouflaged
myself in lust
before love
unveiled me
and made
me a fool.

when you met her

you shook the tree
of my longing
and caught every leaf.
when winter came,
you no longer sat
underneath me.

suddenly the earth tones
clinging to the flesh
of my bones
couldn't compete
with the beauty
and geometry
of a snowflake.

nothing

i chiseled away
parts of myself
trying to be
everything to you
until it could no longer
be rendered as art.

when we fell apart
at the seams,
you howled at me
like i was the moon
and said that i
meant nothing to you.

pangea

you ruptured
the love lakes
of my longing
and scattered
the continents
of my heart.

you told me not to
fall in love with you
but you knew
the contours
of my heart.

smoke

they say that
patience is a virtue
but they never tell you
that the heat of
waiting will burn you
if you linger too long.

sinking

our foundation is rocky
because we made a home
in each other's skin.
we are caving in.
the damage is
beginning to show.

the cracks in the walls
are more prominent
than the ones that
were once in your smile
and my heart has buckled
under the weight of my tears.

i've closed other doors
in an attempt to be yours
but you're always
eyeing the window
and i can't cure
your wandering lust.

paralyzer

i have stars in my
eyes for a guy who would
rather suffocate
and dim them because
they burned bright with love.
he fossilizes
my hopes underneath
his skin to keep from
unearthing my heart.

scavenger

i took all the pieces
i could get from you
and made it look like love.

i hid in the shadows
until you summoned
my light.
i became the sun.

i put out fires you spewed
and cooled you down
with my tongue.
i became a fire-eater.

i made excuses for you
and smeared the writing
on the wall before
everyone woke up.
i became a magician.

i became everything
and everyone but myself.

gentrified

you want to look
into my eyes
when we make love
but i am afraid
you'll see that
i'm the haunted house
no one wants to visit
unless it's halloween.

the forest green
of your eyes
is now the grass.
your skin is the
white picket fence.
your smile is the garden.
you've stripped
my interior
and exterior
and painted them
with your kisses.

i don't know
who i am anymore.
you smell
like gentrification.

barrier

i watch you sleep
and long to hold you
but fear barricades me.
i peacefully retreat,
hold my tears hostage
and force them to drown
the deep and shallow parts
of my heart.

tunnel vision

this love is deferred.
my visions of love
are astigmatic
and blurred
but i still can't take
my eyes off you.

invasion

you've invaded
my solitude
and veins.

the rhythm
of my heart
has not been
the same.

in all my reveries
i tune my breath
to suit your melody.

when words
become obsolete,
i will follow
the echoes
of your heartbeat.

in another life

you say
you crave me
but deprive
yourself of me.

your hunger
mesmerizes me.

hold my hair
as i regurgitate
our past lives
because the way
you breathe on me
feels too familiar.

alchemy

i knew his heart
was yours
but i wanted
to become
an alchemist
to make gold
of the pieces
i received
because
all i ever felt
was the dark side
of his leaded heart.

emissions

sometimes i choke
on the smoke
of our unfiltered
moments.
passion confers
as i breathe you in
but you waste me
like carbon
as i emit my love
to the purple haze
of yesteryear.

missing you

i miss the way
you ripened the fruit
of my inhibitions
and pressed them
into wine.

i miss searching for
my mother tongue
in every kiss.

i miss your fingernails
tracing the veins
of my scattered lineage.

germination

my bruised ego
trips and bears
the fruit of regret.

i am ashamed
to claim the seed
that refused to grow

so i swallow
my feelings whole
on an empty stomach,
expel them
onto blank pages,
and hope something
will bloom inside of me.

epiphany

gun & broom

you jumped
the broom
after you swept
me away like trash.

her grass seemed
greener until
a drought came
and cracked the earth
beneath you.

her eyes burned
brighter until they
ran out of fuel
and left you stranded.

you jumped
the gun
but i dodged
a bullet.

rumor has it
her new husband
is tending
to her yard now.
don't come knocking
on my door!

i am mine

the other day
i saw someone
who reminded
me of you.

time and
my breath
stood still.

as he took
a slow drag
on a cigarette,
i wished
it was my lips
burning at the end
and filling his lungs.

i wanted to be
his craving
and cancer.

in the beginning,
all i wanted was
to be yours.
it took time to realize
that i must stop
giving myself away
as if i didn't belong
to myself.

renewal

when did you construct
this forest of shame?

why did you weaponize your body
and turn it on yourself?

who helped you plant and erect
these toxic thoughts that grew
in the thicket of your reality?

when will you tear it down?
when will you plant love
and forgiveness in its place?

to mothers with scarred daughters

when you see your young daughter
doing womanly things,
do not insult her.
do not let shame
settle in her bones.
she will only seek out others
to stop the rattling—
if only for a moment.

show her some softness.
teach her how to salve
unhealed wounds
by unzipping your silence
and revealing your own—
if only for a moment.

repeat after me

1. it wasn't my fault.

2. i didn't ask for it.

3. consent can be verbal
   and nonverbal.

4. i can withdraw consent
   at any time.

5. the shame is not mine
   to carry.

lost & found

today i will reclaim my body.
i will reach down into the pit
of me and pull out the little girl
who wanted to crawl
into a hole and die.
i will command her to live
and as cliché as it sounds,
i will tell her that it gets better.
that life won't always be
shrouded in darkness.
that she isn't broken
beyond repair.
that there's light at the end
of the tunnel if she would
just open her eyes.

rose quartz

i often wander
into my heart
and gaze through
rose-colored
spectrums.

i often wonder
if your heart
has enough hues
to be human.

don't move.

we can take turns
healing each other.

your belly
is too full
of my love
and i'm always
starving for yours.

self-sabotage

healing requires
every cell
in your body
but i'm so used
to dealing
with myself
in fragments.

sometimes i lift
the scab to revisit
the pink flesh of pain
to feel more alive.

i don't know
who i am
without this bitter
harvest of pain.

would i know
what peace looked like
if it gently knocked
on my heart?

would i open
the door
or pretend
i wasn't home?

true colors

i am beyond the pale.
my kinky hair,
broad nose,
and full lips
are remnants
of my ancestors.

my pride swells
like yeast
in the heat
of your prejudice.

when i found out my hue
prevented you
from choosing me,
i finally saw
your true colors.

sistas in the hooded sky

burnt brass.
honey hued.
draped in midnight
and all its stars.
you are beautiful
just the way you are.
don't let anyone
tell you different.

you are not made of stone.
you are a soft place to land.
you are not a bed of thorns.
you are in full bloom
and need watering too.
don't let anyone
tell you different.

we are more than
our unholy history.
we are a beautiful tapestry
of resilience, sisterhood,
and hope.
i won't let anyone
tell us different.

tornado

i knew you were a tornado
of a man but i gave you
permission to violently swirl
into my heart
and rip off the roof
of my mouth
with your kisses.

loving you was
a natural disaster.
i'm sifting through
the wreckage
to find pieces
of my broken heart
but i will rebuild.

i will raise the foundation
and fill in the gaps with love.

i will lay down rose petals
in the place of your thorns.

i will build walls that won't
tremble when i hear your name.
i will be impenetrable.

lost

i was so preoccupied
with loving you
that i failed
to love myself.

your eyes
became my sight.
your mouth
held my breath.
your body became
my sanctuary.

when it was over
i didn't know
who i was anymore.

i was left blind,
breathless and
aimlessly wandering.

to be honest,
i didn't know
who i was before
but i must
do the work
to find out.

panhandler

i won't become a beggar
standing on the cluttered
corner of your mind
begging for reciprocity.
i will pull my heart
by the strings and walk away.

i will find a love
i won't have to fight
tooth and nail for.
i now know that love
is not warfare.
i will no longer bleed
myself dry for you
or anyone else.

certain men

there are men
who will come to you
late in the night
and hide you
from the light of day
as if you are a vampire.
but they're the ones
holding you down,
biting your neck,
and sucking
all they can
of your veins
until you're lifeless
from loving them.

there are men
who can smell
your insecurity
lynching
every fiber
of your being.
they'll devour you
and claim
you're the sweetest
yet strangest fruit
they have ever tasted.
but they'll never
untie you
because once you
hit the ground,
you'll realize
you deserve more.

there are men
who will come alive
when they're inside of you
but will say you're dead
to them when you step
outside their boundaries.
you'll have to learn
how to balance yourself
on eggshells
before you end up
with egg on your face.

if you ever meet them,
run until your feet
are blistered.
never let them clench
you with their teeth.
you deserve so much better.

when they stop calling

when they stop calling,
do not take your shoes off
and make yourself at home
in the corridors of despair.

do not beg them to retrace
the atlas of your body
in hopes they will discover
something worthy of
exploring and loving.

do not resent your reflection
or question your worth.
you have always
been enough.

this land

this land is heavy.
full of rolling hills
and lush valleys.
not a swollen apology
seeking forgiveness.

i won't apologize for being
a full-bodied woman.
there will be many who
won't be worthy of trekking
or staying.

i will not share this land
with those who keep me
behind closed doors.
with those who walk several
paces before or after me
when someone prettier or
thinner passes by.

i will not share this land
with those who love me
in segments.
you must be able to handle
this vast vessel in the light
and in all its glory.

soft

i must find ways
to be soft
without
using my body.

without
wearing my heart
on my sleeve
for wolves to feed on.

without
hardening parts
of me that scream
for it the most.

when you're feeling low

your mental health
is as delicate
as porcelain.
it only takes
one misstep
for it to shatter
and make you feel
like shards of nothingness.

there are days
you'll wish
to un-breathe
every breath,
unopen your eyes
and fade into black.

i beg of you
to keep filling
your lungs with air.
line the darkness
with stars until
the sun rises again.
your heart of gold
will repair
the broken pieces.

published

i abandoned my words
because you did not like
the sound of them.
to you they were
a profane prayer
for which i wailed on
bloodied bended knees
to be answered.

so i buried them deep
but this book
of ache and longing
collapsed from its spine
and found you and me
hiding underneath
the weight of the words.

it's time to set
these pages free
and i don't give a damn
how you feel about it.

waves

you navigate
the waves
of my emotions.

i try not to linger
but my fingers
ache to touch you.

i'll lie on my side
and wait for your tide
to rush through.

i knew the cause
and effect
of my makeshift beliefs.

i was bound
to drown but
the warrior in me
prevailed.

unlearn

i must turn my back on you
instead of arching it.

i must get you out of my veins
instead of plunging you deeper.

i must remain solid
and not carelessly melt
in the heat of us.

i must drown every memory
of you swimming in my heart.

the burial

you said
i was dead
to you
and buried me
and every memory.

i scurried
to the surface
and offered truth
as reprieve
but you shoveled
more dirt on me.

i never felt
more alive
and dead
at the same time.

refugee

where should i go?
your skin is the only
place i know.
it's a shallow grave
i'll never stop
bringing flowers to.
it's in my bloodline
to honor the dead.

lesson learned

i was willing
to learn our pieces
to make us whole.

i grasped
and strangled
every hope
and endured the
asphyxiation of love.

i've learned
to breathe
without you.
exit my wounds
so i can heal.

search party

love ridden
i searched for you
in corridors,
open doors,
and in endless seas
of similes
and metaphors,
but we never were
on the same page.

colonista

i forged
states of felicity
and found colonies
in our nothingness.

i declared my body
as the flag,
the swirl of our tongues
as the language,
and our love sounds
as the national anthem.

but you rebelled.
you tore into
my heartland
and pledged allegiances
to other territories.

i had to abdicate
my love for you
so i could start
loving myself.

remedy

the art of
letting you go
hasn't been
a graceful one.

i've stumbled,
scraped my knees,
and sought you to heal
the very wounds
you inflicted.

my denial was louder
than the sun.
you were never
my remedy.

the chaos of longing

this voyage—
the chaos
of longing
is no longer
anchored at sea.

i've sailed
the desolate shore
of your heart
and got swept away
by your arctic current.

i floated to the surface
with my heart's
message in a bottle.
i survived you.

dear daddy

i hope you've found
a piece of paradise
that you couldn't find
standing still or
chasing pavements
here on earth.

i hope you took
the biggest bite
and didn't share
with anyone else.

i hope you've laid
down your machete
and wiped the sweat from
your forehead.
you don't have to fight
anymore.

i hope the congested traffic
has left your eyes
and you're able to see
the shades of blue
caressing the sky
and feel the warmth
of the sun.

ordered

there is chaos
in our bones.
grind them
into ashes.
cry over them
until they're dissolved.

if you're all cried out,
find the nearest
body of water
that swells in salt.

repeat until
the chaos
comes into order.
heal.

self-love

if you eat men
and still feel
like you're starving,
you're craving something
that they cannot give.

don't expect men
to fill vessels
that were gifted
to you to overflow.

darling,
find passion
and self-worth within
instead of locking them
inside of men
who like swallowing keys
to keep you to themselves.

elements ii

there's a universe
swirling inside you.

you have to learn to be
your own earth,
wind, fire,
and water.

you are a natural
phenomenon—
not a natural disaster.

glutton

you can't stuff yourself
alive with lust
to fill the empty spaces.

if you love yourself first,
your heart will always be
at full capacity—

not a blinking vacancy sign
that reeks of loneliness,
filth, and despair.

stillness

don't stay
in a moment
for too long.
you tend
to lose yourself.

darling,
you must
be tired
of feeling
your way out
of the dark
long after
they've left.

it's time to
find the light.

devotee

you can't make
anyone love you
no matter how
many times
and ways
you lay down
your body,
your heart,
and your world
at their feet.

they will only
step over you
until they're ready
for you to wash
their feet with your hair
and to set them on fire
with your tongue.

they can tell
by the look
in your eyes
and the way you
surrender
when you part
your thighs
that you deify them.

truth

when you find
your voice,
keep it.
hold it close like
your very first
teddy bear.

swell with pride
with each letter
pressed against pages
that broke
the levees
in your throat

don't shrink
your truth
to make it fit
nicely and neatly
in others
like it's origami.

unfold and
free yourself.

self-love ii

self-love is a journey.
sometimes you must take it
in the heat of the day.
you will find yourself
on the side of the road
thirsty, sweaty,
and out of breath.

you will crave
instant gratification.
you will want to slither
your way back to your choice
of poison, throw your head
back, and take a desperate gulp
because their skin is all you
know.

please don't.
it's time to learn
new things.

it's time to give the love
you denied yourself
but frantically searched
for in others.
it's time to realize that
love was never trapped
underneath their fingertips.
you held it hostage
the entire time.

one day

i will peel the husk
of my insecurities,
soak them
in salt water
and lay them to rest.

i owe this to myself.

the galaxy is yours

star your own sky.
drink the shooting stars.
lasso the moon.
take a bite.
feel the juice
of self-love
running
down your chin
and laugh madly.

you're still alive.
you're still alive.
you're still alive.

index

inception

longing

chaos

epiphany

acknowledgments

To my mother: Thank you for the gift of vulnerability. When I secretly read your letters to God as a child, it gave me the courage to tell my own truths.

To a special person who shall remain nameless: You told me once to "ignite the fire that is creativity, for you are creativity." I've never forgotten those words or you.

To my sisters and close friends: Thank you for believing in me when I didn't believe in myself. Your faith propels me.

To my muses: I gathered our severed pieces and gave them a place to rest. These are artifacts from our past lives. Handle them with care.

about the author

K.Y. Robinson is an introverted writer based in Houston, Texas. She received a B.A. in journalism and M.A. in history from Texas Southern University. She has loved words pressed against pages since childhood and has been chasing them ever since. *The Chaos of Longing* is her first published poetry collection.

Robinson draws from personal experiences as a woman of color, trauma and mental illness survivor, and hopeless romantic.

For updates, please visit kyrobinson.net.

Andrews McMeel Publishing
a division of Andrews McMeel Universal
1130 Walnut Street, Kansas City, Missouri 64106

www.andrewsmcmeel.com

17 18 19 20 21 BVG 10 9 8 7 6 5 4 3 2

ISBN: 978-1-4494-9203-8

Library of Congress Control Number: 2017947146

Editor: Melissa Rhodes
Art Director, Designer: Holly Swayne
Production Editor: David Shaw
Production Manager: Cliff Koehler

Cover design by Kat Savage
Cover illustration by Angga Agustiya

ATTENTION: SCHOOLS AND BUSINESSES
Andrews McMeel books are available at quantity discounts with bulk purchase for educational, business, or sales promotional use. For information, please e-mail the Andrews McMeel Publishing Special Sales Department: specialsales@amuniversal.com.